Create an Exciting New Start

Don M. Haney

NEWMAN SPRINGS PUBLISHING
320 Broad Street
Red Bank, NJ 07701

First originally published by Newman Springs Publishing 2024

ISBN 979-8-89308-196-1 (Paperback)
ISBN 979-8-89308-197-8 (Digital)

Printed in the United States of America

Contents

Preface

J. K. Rowling said it better than I can. She said, "Failure gave me an inner security that I have never attained by passing examinations. Failure taught me things about myself that I could have learned no other way." While she was writing *Harry Potter and the Sorcerer's Stone*, she was divorced, had a daughter, had no job, and was living in government housing. But she did have an old typewriter. She became a multimillionaire within five years. She said, "The knowledge that you have emerged wiser and stronger from setbacks means that you are, ever after, secure in your ability to survive. You will never truly know yourself or the strength of your relationships until both have been tested by adversity. Such knowledge is a true gift, for all that it is painfully won, and it has been worth more than any qualification that I have ever earned." Make the worst thing that ever happened to you the best thing that ever happened to you.

I've had to change industries three times. It wasn't because I was doing a bad job. It was because the industries changed. I've won national, regional, and district sales contests. One year, I opened at least one new account for fifty consecutive weeks. Then, when I found an industry that I could stay in for a while, I developed a voice disorder, which isn't a great thing when you work in sales. I've made adjustments and learned how to get people to listen to what I'm saying instead of how I'm saying it. I'm able to stay calm and composed even when I have to repeat things several times. Many times, I have to rephrase things to get someone to understand what I'm saying. People realize that I know what I want to say. It's just a struggle for me to talk.

Fifteen years after developing a voice disorder, I started pioneering a new line of custom products in my territory. I've sold to some of my previous customers, but most of the sales with the new line are to people that I've never spoken with before. And this line takes a lot of explanation. In the second year representing the new line, I made more money with the new line than I did with my other two lines.

I'm no expert and I'm not perfect by any means. But I've had to start over. Since I've been on a similar journey to yours, I'm like your guide on the side, pointing out the slippery slopes. Sometimes we learn more from failure than from success. Learn from it and keep moving. There are winners and learners. I'm hoping to inspire you to do better than what I've done. My mission is to empower you to turn your test into a testimonial. If you want to learn from my battle scars, keep reading.

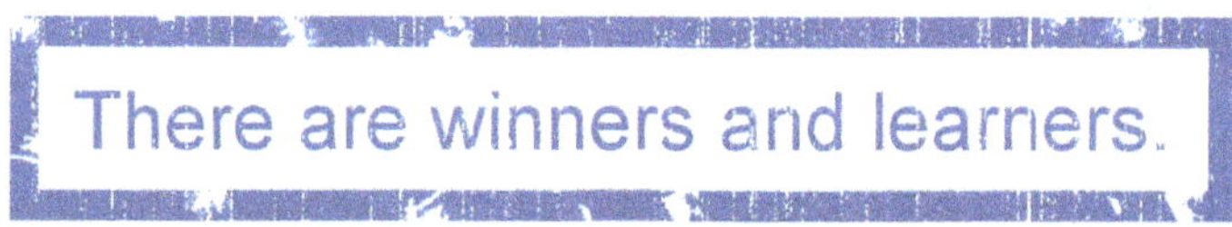

Introduction

According to the Resilience Alliance, resilience is the most important factor when adapting to change. You have to maintain high levels of performance even in times of change.

In athletics, that's called being clutch. Can you perform in the clutch, or will the pressure get to you? If you can perform in the clutch, you will grow stronger rather than feel defeated by the experience.

That's what this book is about. I hope it helps you create an exciting new start.

Now Is the Time to Reinvent Yourself

Constantly focusing on the stress isn't going to help you. Define your big-picture goals and take action.

Have a goal and a game plan every day. Be consistent and keep showing up. Document the process. Celebrate small successes along the way.

Has the coronavirus pandemic forced you to think differently about what you want to do in your life? When your life gets turned upside down, it creates an opportunity to invent a new life.

If you were to claim what you really want, what would that be? If you can see what you want, you can create it.

Are you really going to go back where you were? That job or that business may not be available when we come out of this. Even if you could go back, is that where you want to be? Or do you see a new opportunity?

Have a willingness to evolve. Allow yourself to change your focus. Where is the opportunity for you? How can you evolve to a better place? How can you improve and change?

Maybe you always wanted to do something else. Now you are free to do it.

This is the moment when you get to change everything. If there's anything you've put on hold, now is the time to pursue it. Use this as fuel and discipline to get it done.

We're not going to come out of this coronavirus pandemic in the same place as before. The best time to reinvent yourself is now. Let's go!

It's not where you start.
It's where you finish that counts.

7 Tips for Job Hunting in the Age of COVID-19

Whether you just graduated from college or you've been working for years, the coronavirus pandemic has likely turned your life upside down. Many things will never be the same.

Virtual work and job hunting have become the norm as you deal with intense economic uncertainty.

It's normal to feel discouraged now, but there are steps you can take to boost your chances of landing a job.

1.   Look for growing industries

Not all industries are struggling right now. Some are growing. Many are busier than ever and need to hire to keep up with demand.

Remote working platforms like Zoom and Slack are booming. Food retailers such as Target and supermarkets are busy.

Logistics and insurance are going digital and need employees with different skill sets.

E-commerce is growing.

Travel, hospitality, and entertainment are significantly down. Look for industries that are hiring more than firing.

2.   Be flexible

You might need to change your plans to adapt to these changing circumstances. You might need to be less picky about the role you want and focus on finding a position where you can learn valuable skills.

Don't disregard an opportunity just because it's different from what you imagined. It might help you develop skills that you'll use throughout your career.

3. Lean on your network

Reach out to people in your network, like professors, alumni, and friends. Develop your relationships and get referrals for jobs.

During the coronavirus pandemic, you might not be able to attend job fairs or networking events, but you can still network online.

4. Highlight your remote-work skills

With all the office closures, if you can show hiring managers that you have the skills to work remotely and without supervision, that may give you the edge you need to stand out among job candidates.

Some of this is challenging, but it's also creating new opportunities for jobs and careers.

5. Revamp your résumé

While you're spending time at home these days, make the most of it by revamping your résumé, cover letter, portfolio, and other job materials.

It's usually better if you tailor your résumé for each position rather than send a generic one to all prospective employers.

Use keywords from the job description in your résumé. That will show that you've done your homework. It could also help your resume pass an applicant tracking system.

Some employers use software to vet applications by scanning for keywords. Seventy-five percent of résumés are rejected by machines without ever being looked at by a person.

Even if you don't have much experience yet, you can highlight your involvement in school clubs, volunteer work, internships, or course projects that might impress a hiring manager.

6.   *Create your online presence*

Of course, you need to delete any pictures or comments that you don't want a prospective employer to see. In some industries, up to 95 percent of recruiters have reported using social media to vet candidates.

Beef up your professional LinkedIn profile. Show endorsements. Use bullet points under each job to focus on your accomplishments.

You could author blog posts to amplify your voice on LinkedIn and build your personal brand. An online portfolio or website might help for some job targets.

7.   *Focus on the long game*

You might be impatient about getting your career started or restarted, but remember that very few people get their dream job right out of the gate. And it might take longer now because of the coronavirus pandemic.

Don't lose hope.

The current setback is worldwide. Things look different now from what anyone imagined, but that doesn't mean it will always be this way. Keep focusing your efforts and moving forward.

A side hustle or temporary work now could be a stepping stone that gets you closer to your destination.

Tell yourself these ten two-letter words:

If it is to be, it is up to me.

7 Tips to Master a Video Interview

1. *Master technology.* Make sure that you're familiar and comfortable with the technology you're going to be using so that you'll get excellent results.

2. *Center the camera at eye level.* Your face should be the focal point of the screen.

3. *Choose your location carefully.* A room with the door closed is ideal. Make sure it's quiet and well lit. Try to keep the background simple, avoiding clutter or distractions.

4. *Dress professionally.* Dress as you would for an in-person interview. You can't go wrong dressing in dark colors. Avoid loud colors or patterns that might distract.

5. *Watch your body language.* In a live interview, you would look into the interviewer's eyes. In this case, look at the camera to make your eyes appear centered on the screen for the interviewer.

6. *Stay focused and engaged.* Don't look around the room while gathering your thoughts, as it can give the impression of disengagement.

7. *Critique your performance.* After each interview, critique every nuance while it's still fresh in your mind. Write down the questions and your answers. Were your answers short and to the point? Were you satisfied with your responses? If you could do it over, what would you change?

8. *Practice makes perfect.* Get a coworker or a friend to do practice interviews with you. The more you practice, the better you'll get. Not only will your answers be more polished, but you'll also gain confidence.

It's your time to *stand out*!

Why You Should Start a Side Hustle Now

Has there ever been an easier time to start a side hustle? We live in the golden age of side hustling.

If you need some extra money to pay off debt, save more, or even buy that shiny new thing you've been wanting, there's really no excuse why you can't do it now.

Compare the nature of the side hustle today to just a few years ago. There wasn't a sharing economy or an on-demand economy.

Making extra money meant either finding a part-time job or figuring out a way to make your own job. Finding a part-time job meant working when your boss told you to work.

That's a problem for people who want flexibility. And creating your own job meant figuring out a skill you had and finding customers, not to mention probably needing to spend some money to get your side hustle started.

In contrast, look at the wealth of options available today.

There are entire marketplaces on the Internet where you can sell goods and services without needing to make the jump into starting a full-fledged business.

If you want to make some extra money on the side, then you are living in the right time in history. The ability to work whenever or wherever you want is the biggest reason we are in the golden age of side hustling.

Has there ever been a time when you could choose to work at any moment of the day whenever you felt like it?

Or when you could earn money basically doing things you are already doing and using skills you already have?

There's no need to pick up a second job or work any set schedules. You don't need to work full days. You don't even need to work full hours at a time.

Technology has also greatly decreased barriers to entry to the point where there are almost none if you're looking to start a side hustle.

It isn't like a job. You don't have to interview for it. Mostly, you just sign up and get started.

You can have a self-sufficient money-making opportunity up and running in just a few hours.

Given how easy it is to get started on a side hustle, why on earth would you not have at least one set up?

If you need help, here's a cool book that's so informative and motivating. It's called *What If It Does Work Out? How a Side Hustle Can Change Your Life* by Susie Moore. You can buy the book in hardcover or softcover for less than $15 on Amazon.

> Is today the day to begin new projects and a new way of life that truly inspires you? (Jonathan Lockwood Huie)

> In the middle of difficulty lies opportunity. (Albert Einstein)

A Chance Conversation Opened My Eyes

I went to a meeting where the president and the chairman of the Board of Regents were going to talk with the alumni. I arrived about thirty minutes early, picked up my name tag, and I went over to the table where the water pitchers were since I hadn't had anything to drink in a while. I heard a woman talking to a man where the iced tea was. I heard her say that she works in a school, but I didn't hear what she does.

When the president and the chairman came in, I talked to both. I told the president what I wanted to say. (She was impressed that I had already listened to the recordings of the five previous meetings online.) I asked the chairman the question I wanted to ask him.

I looked around and noticed the woman was sitting by herself. She had seemed very friendly when she was talking to the man near where I was standing. So I walked over there and asked if she was saving a seat for anyone. She said no. Her purse was in the chair next to her, so I sat in the next chair. Her name is Melody.

I said, "My throat has really been bothering me all day, so I am just going to sit down." For some reason, it seemed easier talking with her. I guess that it was because we were alone, and I didn't have to talk over anyone else.

Melody asked, "Do you need a lozenge or something?"

I said, "It's not like that. I have a voice disorder called spasmodic dysphonia that makes my vocal cords stick together. Today, I was having trouble talking with everyone."

She was really interested. She works with kids in her school that have speaking problems.

Melody asked, "Have you seen an ear, nose, and throat specialist?"

I said, "They can't help. If you look at my vocal cords, they look fine. And doctors want to say that it's just laryngitis. Among people with spasmodic dysphonia, it's a joke. 'Yeah, I've had laryngitis for twenty years.'"

She laughed at that.

Melody asked, "Have you tried voice therapy exercises?"

I said, "I have, but the whole focus is to get you to speak from your diaphragm. That's not the problem. It's sticking in my vocal cords. It's in the same family as tremors. It's muscles that spasm. Instead of tremors, my vocal cords stick together."

Melody asked, "Is there anything that can be done?"

I said, "There's surgery, but I've known some people who had the surgery. It takes about six months to get back to speaking. I work in sales. I can't afford to take off six months."

Melody said, "I'm not for surgery either."

I said, "I've adjusted and just worked through it. The strange thing is that people are listening to me more now than they did when I had a decent voice. I'm smiling more and using my hands more and using inflections more. Maybe that helps."

Melody said, "I think people are listening more because they realize that it's a struggle for you to talk, so they're focusing more on what you're saying."

I said, "And they realize that I do have something relevant to say. I think that it probably helps that I'm able to stay calm and composed regardless of how many times I must repeat things."

We went on to talk about some stuff related to our alma mater, and a male friend came to sit by her. She moved her purse and sat by me. She introduced him to me. His name is Michael. And she showed him the card that I had given her. He had never heard of spasmodic dysphonia either.

After the meeting was over, I told Melody that I had a couple of things to tell her and a question for her. I told her two things about the president and the chairman.

Melody was getting ready to leave.

I said, "I think that I was supposed to sit by you."

With a big smile, Melody said, "Yeah, you were supposed to sit by me."

I said, "I want to go back to why you said that people are listening to me better. You said that it's because they realize that it's a struggle for me to talk."

Melody said, "When I am working with kids, I lean closer. I try to read their lips. I look at their eyes. I try to get clues other than their words."

I said, "That does happen to me. People get closer and closer to me. When they see that I want to say something to them, they will walk over to me and lean in to hear what I have to say. They know that I'm going to make a relevant comment or ask a relevant question. And they know that they need to be close to understand me.

"Over the last few weeks, I've been trying to figure out why people are listening to me more now. Logically, it doesn't make sense. Voice gets worse, and people listen better. I feel like I've got a story to tell. I've changed industries three times. Then, when I find an industry that I can stay in for a while, I start losing my voice, and I must adjust to that.

"I didn't want to walk up to a customer or someone that I talk with a lot at ball games and ask them why they are listening to me. I've talked to some new prospects recently, and they were listening to me. I had never talked to the president or the chairman before. They were both listening to me. And they got very close to me to hear me."

I didn't tell her why I chose to sit by her. I was trying to help her feel like she belonged.

Yet she told me the very answer that I'd been trying to figure out. I can't tell my story (in writing, of course) if I don't know what's happening.

At first, it's like, "What's wrong with this guy?" I was getting hung up on that look when people first hear me speak. I must repeat myself so often that it seems normal. I'm surprised if I go through a day without having to repeat myself. But I never change the tone of my voice. It's not their fault that they can't understand me.

At some point, they realize that I'm trying the best I can, and I'm going to keep talking until I'm sure they get it. And then they start trying harder to understand me.

I had to learn to convey the message that "I'm okay. I just have a voice problem. I'm more than a bad voice." But I don't say that. I'm just sending that message through nonverbal signs or in attitude.

I certainly didn't go to that meeting expecting help from a voice coach, but that's exactly what I got.

*****

Last year, a hit-and-run accident happened right in front of me. The young lady, Stephanie, was freaking out. I called her over.

I said, "Here's my phone number. I'll be your witness for the insurance company."

We were waiting for a deputy. She asked me to stay with her, and I said that I would. Stephanie was down. She had gotten a divorce and moved in with her parents.

Suddenly, a guy drove up in a sports car. He said that the driver crashed her car on his street after hitting Stephanie. And the deputy wanted us to drive over to the site of the second crash.

So we followed the sports car to his street.

When we got there, there were several people who had witnessed the second crash. While we were waiting for the deputy to take our reports, we were talking to all the people at the second site.

I said, "Stephanie, look around. There are more people trying to help you than trying to hurt you."

How to Use Body Language to Build Trust

I've been doing these things for as long as I can remember, and I think that I concentrated more on body language and smiling after developing a voice disorder. I think that's why people are listening to me more now than they did when I had a decent voice. And that's why people can understand me better in person than on the phone. You can use these tips if you're trying to get hired or if you're trying to make a sale. Trust is at the core of every type of human transaction, whether it's business or personal. Generally, we don't like people we don't trust. And we tend to trust people we like.

Using body language is the best way to get people to trust you. The body communicates how you feel about yourself and the way you feel about other people. We're communicating with people before a word is spoken. The following tips will help you use body language to build trust:

1. *Have a genuine, heartfelt smile.* This lets people know they can relax and feel safe with you. Practice smiling when you greet people, and pay attention to the positive impact on others.

2. *Smile when encouraging people.* When you're praising, complimenting, or congratulating someone, do it with a smile. It magnifies your message and makes it more memorable.

3. *If you're meeting someone or ending a conversation, a strong, confident handshake is essential.* The physical action makes it more memorable.
4. *Make eye contact when shaking hands.* Always look the other person in the eyes before ending a handshake. It makes you seem charismatic.
5. *When listening, make eye contact with the person that's speaking.* Looking at someone and actually listening (instead of thinking of what you want to say) makes an invisible connection between you and the speaker.
6. *When you look at someone more than 60 percent of the time, it signals that you're interested and that they matter.*
7. *Mirror the speaker's sentiments.* Nodding and reflecting their emotions show the speaker that you're following along and that their words have an effect on you. Of course, if you're really listening, then you can comment on what they just said. That will really confirm that you were listening and interested in what they were saying.

Using these body language cues gives people reassurance and wins their trust. They will view you as a genuine person who is sincerely interested in them. You'll build strong, lasting impressions that will help you make friends and allies.

Building Relationships and Developing Trust

I've been a sales representative since 1978. There's never been a single time that I've worried about someone catching me in a lie. Not my customers. Not the companies that I represent. If a customer gives me a check, the company will release their next order as soon as I tell them that I've got a check. I've never said that the check is in the mail if I wasn't going to mail it.

That's not the case with our customers. With customers, we don't believe that the check is in the mail until the check arrives because so many customers lie to us. But if I say that I'm mailing a check, they will release the order because I always mail the checks when I say that I'm mailing a check.

Occasionally, a customer will try to say that I told them something that's not true, to which I'll say, "No, I didn't." I'll then show them the prices and quantity discounts in the catalog. I'll show them a copy of their order. I'll tell them that I left an order copy with them or faxed an order copy to them or emailed an order copy to them. I don't have to try to remember what I told them. I use the prices that are printed in the catalogs. I can always look back at the catalog and see what prices I used.

Usually, someone will only try to fool me once or twice. They realize that I can back up what I say. So when I'm being introduced to a new buyer, manager, or assistant, they say something like "We buy this and this from Don. You can trust him. He's a nice guy."

I'm not tossing and turning at night because I'm worried about what someone might say about me. I've built relationships and developed trust.

There's another thing about being honest. If I walk into a room, and they say, "We were just talking about you," I don't think, *Oh my gosh! What were they saying?* I say, "Oh really? What were you talking about?"

Despite what you might have heard, good money can be made from serving your customers, not exploiting them. And you can sleep well at night.

Choosing to Be Happy

I was two and a half years old when my oldest younger sister was born. I remember my father's parents taking me to the hospital. We stood on the sidewalk while my mother held my sister up to the window.

My grandmother said, "Don, there's your sister."

I don't remember anything before that. It's like my life started that day.

I've seen pictures of the house where we lived when I was born. I've seen pictures of the dog they had when I was born. I don't remember any of that.

My parents were very negative and critical. My father died when I was sixty. I received a total of three compliments from my father. That's three more than I got from my mother. I never did anything good enough. But they also told me, "You're old enough to do it yourself." That probably didn't start when I was two and a half. But it seems like I heard that my whole life.

It might have started when my second younger sister was born. I was four and a half then. It just seems like I was always told that I can't do anything right but old enough to do things by myself.

I was twelve and a half when my youngest sister was born. My parents kept going to all their club and church activities because I was old enough to babysit. I was old enough to babysit, but I couldn't do anything right.

When I started driving, I would take my two oldest sisters to their activities. I was old enough to take them places and pick them up, but I couldn't do anything right.

In truth, my parents didn't want to stay home with the kids. Whatever time I freed up by helping with my sisters was time they could be doing other things.

Is it any wonder that I have worked more than forty years in wholesale sales? I didn't want someone looking over my shoulder while I was working. I wanted to set my own schedule. And I was old enough to do it myself.

Just pay me commission for what I sold.

Looking back on it now, I could have carried all that baggage with me when I went to school, and I could have been bullied.

But I didn't.

I enjoyed being away from my parents. I wanted to talk with people. And I wanted to do my own thing. I learned quickly and made good grades.

Most of the students liked me.

In fact, I talked too much in school. I would talk to anyone who sat around me. My worst grades were in conduct. I wasn't really disruptive, like throwing things at the teacher or pulling girls' hair. I was just friendly with everyone around me.

It might have helped that I was one of the bigger kids. My father and his relatives were all stocky. I took after that side of the family.

My father had a wholesale milk business. I don't remember when I started helping him on the milk truck. It seemed like I always did. I was probably working with him as soon as I was old enough to carry something into the stores.

A full case of milk weighed fifty-five pounds. We would often carry five or six cases on a two-wheel cart. There were no handicap ramps back then. If there were steps going into the stores, we pulled the cart up the steps.

When I was in high school, I got a commercial driver's license so I could drive the milk truck. I couldn't do anything right, but I could drive the truck with a full load of milk. Does that make any sense? It's surprising that I'm somewhat sane.

I was a stocky kid that was used to carrying cases of milk into the stores. That probably helped with the way that I carried myself; I never walked around with my head down, so I probably didn't appear to be a good target for bullying.

But I think it was because I chose to be happy. Why mess with the happy kid who wants to talk with everybody?

Apparently, I was like this from day one in school. I had two girlfriends in kindergarten. I was able to separate home and school.

When I was in high school, I played football and baseball. I didn't have any speed, so I was an offensive lineman in football and a catcher in baseball. In my senior year, I was a starter on both the football and baseball varsity teams.

There was teasing on those teams, but I never was bullied.

During my freshman year in college, I decided to join a fraternity. The members always yelled at the pledges. I would just smile and go along with it. I realized they yelled at you more if you messed up. I chose to keep my cool and be happy.

I realized it was all a game. The members knew the rules, and the pledges didn't. If I kept my cool and went along with the game, then they would yell at someone else who messed up.

After weeks of this, one member told me that it wasn't any fun to pick on me because I never got shook up. I just smiled. That was my plan all along. Choose to be happy, regardless of what the members said.

After college, I worked in retail stores for six years. I started to realize that I would rather have a job like the sales representatives who sold to us.

A sales rep got me an interview with his regional manager. I pointed out that I had worked in different types of retail stores, so I thought that I would be able to sell to different types of stores. He hired me as a trainee.

I've had to change industries and make adjustments as the retail scene changed. I've had great customers and awful customers. But I chose to be happy and kept going with the flow…for more than forty years.

Twenty years ago, I started developing a voice disorder. That's not a good thing when you're in sales, right?

At first, it's kind of a shock when you say something, and people look at you like, "What's wrong with him?" But I still chose to be happy.

I had always tried to be a helpful, knowledgeable salesperson. Having a great voice and telling great stories weren't part of what I did. I was there trying to help them.

I kept making adjustments, and I kept trying to help people. And I honestly think that people are listening to me more now than they did when I had a decent voice. Since they can tell that it's a struggle for me to talk, I guess they appreciate it more that I'm being nice and trying to help them. And I'm still working in sales.

I'm happy, and I try to say something that they want to hear or ask a relevant question. Of course, people have to be close to me to understand what I'm saying. I take it as a compliment that they're stepping close to me so they can understand what I'm saying.

Let me be clear. I'm *not* talking about laughing at a funeral or laughing when someone gets hurt. I still like and care about people.

I'm talking about my mindset. And choosing to be happy has helped me all the way through grades K-12 and in college. It helped me as a sales rep.

It helped me when I developed a voice disorder.

Right now, I will talk to anyone, from the president of the company to the janitor. And both seem to enjoy talking with me. So they will ask me what I said and get closer so they can understand me.

Choosing to be happy will help you too.

Obviously, these are my stories. But I started putting together how choosing to be happy had helped me throughout my life after a VIP coaching call with the Go Big coach, Kristen Howe.

You can join those monthly calls. Go to this link to find out more: www.GoBigCoach.com.

You can ask Kristen questions by email (that's what I do), by raising your hand on the phone, or by typing a question online. I guarantee that she'll answer your question.

Everybody else has a set time for a call or a Zoom meeting, and they'll say, "We have time for one more question."

Kristen isn't like that. Before she ends a call, she'll check to make sure that she's answered every question from emails or live during the call. Check it out.

Choose to be happy!

Are You in the Right Environment?

If you want to raise your standards, you need to raise your environment.

As long as you make excuses, you will be stuck. No matter what someone did or didn't do, it doesn't change who you are. Let go of the old. Get ready for the new. Get rid of the excuses.

As long as you justify your position, you're giving it permission to stay.

Everything you're surrounded by keeps you where you are—your friends, your family, your habits, the media you consume, everything.

You need to be careful who you spend time with. Misery loves company. If you are sick, don't go find other sick people to be around.

If you're addicted, don't hang around people who are addicted.

If you're depressed, don't go find five other people who are depressed.

If you're negative and critical, don't find five other negative, critical people.

Find happy, positive people.

If you're in school, your grades will be the average of the five people you spend the most time with. Find people who have what you want.

I have seven people I listen to or whose works I read regularly. There are others I listen to or whose works I read, but those seven are my regular ones every week.

I can't say that my income is the average of those seven people…yet. But it has affected my attitude. I think more like them. Something will happen, and something one of them has said or written will pop into my head.

Well-meaning people will try to talk you out of your destiny. You need to get away from people who see you as you were and not what you will be.

Sometimes it is people you have known the longest who are the ones that only see you one way—as you were in the past. Since they only see you one way, they put limitations on you.

Nothing that has happened to you can stop your destiny. No sickness, no person, and no event can stop your destiny.

Say to yourself, "This may be where I am, but it's not who I am." Where you come from isn't who you are. You have seeds of greatness in you.

You're not limited by where you come from or what you've done in the past. Don't talk yourself out of it. Don't let circumstances hold you back.

Leave negative mindsets. Leave limitations that other people put on you. Where you start isn't as important as where you finish.

If you take an oak tree seed and plant it in a five-gallon pot, it'll never be the tree that it was supposed to be, and it's not because there's something wrong with the seed. It's in the wrong environment.

You have seeds of greatness. Make sure that your pot isn't too small.

Don't settle for what your parents had or didn't have or what your relatives did or didn't do.

Be around people who inspire you and encourage you. You were made for more.

We can't hold on to the old and expect to receive the new. The past is the past. Life isn't always fair. Don't dwell on it. Don't keep thinking about it. Move on to new things. Move on to a new environment.

The past doesn't have to define you. Bad breaks, the hurt, and the losses don't define you. You were made for more.

Things that have held you back are being broken. You're headed for a new level of freedom and breakthroughs.

Make sure you're not in a five-gallon pot.
Make sure you're in the right environment.

The Oak Tree
By Johnny Ray Ryder Jr.

A mighty wind blew night and day.
It stole the Oak Tree's leaves away.
Then snapped its boughs
and pulled its bark
until the Oak was tired and stark.

But still the Oak Tree held its ground
while other trees fell all around.
The weary wind gave up and spoke,
"How can you still be standing Oak?"

The Oak Tree said, "I know that you
can break each branch of mine in two,
carry every leaf away,
shake my limbs and make me sway.

But I have roots stretched in the earth,
growing stronger since my birth.
You'll never touch them, for you see
they are the deepest part of me.

Until today, I wasn't sure
of just how much I could endure.
But now I've found with thanks to you,
I'm stronger than I ever knew."

Who Am I?

See If You Can Answer This Quiz.

Let's see how smart you are today. Here's a quiz for you.

I am your constant companion. I am your greatest helper or your heaviest burden. I will push you onward or drag you down to failure. I am completely at your command. Half of the things you do, you might as well turn over to me…and I will be able to do them quickly and correctly. I am easily managed; you must merely be firm with me. Show me exactly how you want something done, and after a few lessons, I will do it automatically. I am the servant of all great people and, alas, of all failures as well. Those who are great, I have made great. Those who are failures, I have made failures. I am not a machine, though I work with all the precision of a machine plus the intelligence of a human. You may run me for profit or run me for ruin; it makes no difference to me. Take me, train me, be firm with me, and I will put the world at your feet. Be easy with me, and I will destroy you. Who am I?

I am a habit.

This quiz was written by Michael Senoff, founder of www. HardToFindSeminars.com.

Your Focus Is Your Future

A philosophy professor walked into his classroom with a large empty mayonnaise jar. He filled the jar to the top with large rocks and asked the students if the jar was full.

The students said, "Yes, it is full."

He then added small pebbles to the jar and shook the jar so the pebbles would settle into the spaces around the large rocks. Then he asked the students again if the jar was full now.

The students agreed the jar was full.

The professor then poured sand into the jar to fill up the remaining space.

The students agreed the jar was completely full now.

The professor explained that the jar represents everything that is in one's life. The rocks represent the most important things. The pebbles represent things that matter, but you could live without them if you didn't do those things right now. The sand represents the remaining filler in your life, like material possessions, and time killers like TV, Facebook, email, shopping, or surfing the Internet. We are staying busy, but at the end of the day, have we accomplished anything? Or have we just substituted action for progress?

If you start putting sand in the jar first, you won't have room for the pebbles and the rocks. It's the same with your life. If you spend all of your time on the small, insignificant things, you will run out of time for the things that are important. The rocks are your priorities. The pebbles are somewhat important. The sand is wasting your time.

If you identify the most important things in your life, you can set aside the time to work on those. In the long run, it's okay to procrastinate on the other projects that aren't as important. If you solve the big issues first by putting the rocks into the jar first, the small issues can still fall into place. But, if you put the sand and the pebbles in first, there won't be room for the rocks.

There's *one* word that all of your dreams and goals hinge on. That word is *attention*.

Attention matters in all your dreams and goals, whether it's happiness, success, love, opportunity, peace, or your ideal body weight. To reach your dreams and goals, you must focus your attention on what you desire. It seems simple, doesn't it? But most people don't do that. They focus on what they don't want, and that is what they get.

You can't serve two masters. You are either moving *toward* your dreams and goals, or you are moving *away* from the things you desire. It depends on what you focus your attention on most of the time.

Are the habits that you have today on par with the dreams that you have for tomorrow? A pro has professional habits, and an amateur has amateur habits.

One day in 1918, Charles M. Schwab, the president of a large steel company, met with a respected productivity consultant named Ivy Lee.

Schwab brought Lee into his office and said, "Show me a way to get more things done."

Lee replied, "Give me fifteen minutes with each of your executives."

Schwab asked, "How much will it cost me?"

Lee replied, "Nothing. Unless it works. After three months, you can send me a check for whatever you feel it's worth to you."

Lee returned a few days later. During his fifteen minutes with each manager, he explained a simple daily routine for achieving peak productivity: At the end of each workday, write down the six most important things you need to accomplish tomorrow. Don't write down more than six tasks. Prioritize those six items in order of their true importance. When you arrive tomorrow, concentrate only on the first task. Work until the first task is finished before moving on to the second task. Approach each item the same way. At the end of the day, move any unfinished items to a new list of six tasks for the following day. Repeat this process every workday.

Schwab and his management team decided to give Lee's method a try. After three months, he was so delighted with the progress that he called Lee into his office and wrote him a check for $25,000 (the equivalent of more than $400,000 today).

Try the Ivy Lee method for your life. Your focus is your future. Make the important thing the important thing.

Just Get Up

Scott Hamilton is an Olympic gold medalist, a network-TV skating commentator, an actor, a performer, a producer, a best-selling author, a role model, a humanitarian, a philanthropist, and a cancer and brain tumor survivor.

In his book *The Great Eight: How to Be Happy (Even When You Have Every Reason to Be Miserable)*, Scott wrote,

> In skating, the first thing you learn is how to get up from a fall. Trust me, you will fall. It's as certain a fact as it will be freezing in northern Ohio in February. Coaches teach you how to get up: first, push up on all fours like a dog, then kneel on one leg and push yourself up with your hands to standing. It's not that hard. In fact, it is easier to get up than it is to skate. So why fear falling?
>
> It saddens me that a lot of people don't try new things because they're afraid of falling, whether literally or figuratively. It's a shame. As long as you know how to get up, you have nothing to worry about. It doesn't matter what the challenge is—athletics, business, romance, health, academics, the arts—the rule for getting up is the same: you just get up!

As long as you know how to get up, you have
nothing to worry about. You just get up!

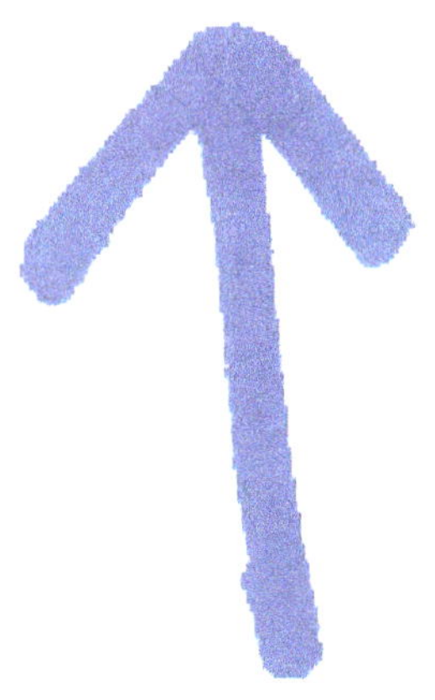

Changing Times— Problem or Opportunity?

Years ago, people would work for the same company for 40 years and receive a gold watch when they retired. It's not like that anymore. The average time at one job now is 4.5 years.

While I was writing this book, it was announced that my wife's boss would be retiring next year. Her boss says that she is "well thought of" in the company. She didn't know if they would find another position for her. But someone else in the executive suites did hire her.

Then I received a phone call from the owner of a company that I have represented for twenty-five years. He told me that the company had been sold and that all of the inventory had been moved to another state. Within a few days, the owner of the old company and the owner of the new company thanked me for my help in the transition.

I chose not to represent the new company. This is better for me because I can focus on the company that I've been representing for two years, where the business is growing.

We've got to be ready to change with the times now.

With closings, sales, mergers, downsizing, outsourcing, and automation, things are changing quickly now. The middle class is being squeezed by stagnant wages that barely keep up with inflation, while costs are rising for health insurance, health care, prescription drugs, childcare, education, vehicles, and seemingly everything else that we have to buy.

It's not what's happening around you, and it's not what's happening to you; what really matters is what's happening inside you.

$$E + R = O$$
Event plus response equals outcome.

Oh yes, the past can hurt, but the way I see it, you can either run from it or learn from it. (Rafiki from *The Lion King*)

Sometimes You Will Need These 7 Words

Because of this, something good will happen.

Deepak Chopra said, "Believe the diagnosis, not the prognosis." The doctors have no idea what will happen.

In the late 1970s, in Wilmington, North Carolina, a player tried out for the varsity basketball team and was cut. He said that was the worst feeling he had ever experienced in his life. That feeling made him work so hard because he never wanted to experience that feeling again. The next year, he made the high school varsity team. Then he played in college and in the NBA. He is Michael Jordan, the greatest player in the history of the NBA.

Have you ever flunked out, been fired, or received a bad prognosis?

Because of this, something good will happen.

How to *Deal* with Events

Eric Heiden achieved the greatest individual Winter Olympic feat when he won five gold medals, set four Olympic records, and set a world record in speed skating at the 1980 Lake Placid Olympics.

He once said, "It's not the events in our life that define our character but how we *deal* with them."

One person on a plane is bored, and another person is having a panic attack. It can't be the plane. It's the response to the plane.

Some players are clutch players, and there are chokers. Clutch players come through in key moments. Chokers don't.

Train yourself to be clutch.

You're always going to have problems. Be a problem solver.

Life is a continuous series of problem-solving events. In approaching a problem, you have a choice. Are you going to be frustrated or fascinated?

When something gets difficult, get charged up. Get more energized. Get more fascinated.

Frustration never works. Fascination always works.

Life is like climbing ladders. You get to the top of one ladder, and you go to another ladder. Make sure that it's against the right wall and where you want to go. Get really good at climbing ladders.

If you like climbing ladders, you'll do well in school, athletics, sales, business, research, whatever you decide to do.

When someone wins an award, you never hear them say, "I'm surprised I won this award. I hate what I do, and I'm always frustrated."

You have to like climbing ladders. The people who are the most successful are the ones who climb the most ladders. And they will have the most skill.

Put passion and skill together, and you'll be very successful.

Get really good at climbing ladders.

Having Trouble Getting Started?

What if you have to write a paper, a report, an assignment, a résumé, or a project, and you don't feel like it?

What if you need to make phone calls, and you don't feel like it?

What if you need to go to the gym or go for a walk, and you don't feel like it?

> The way to get started is to quit talking and begin doing. (Walt Disney)

Use the fifteen-minute rule. Tell yourself you will do it for fifteen minutes. After fifteen minutes, you can decide if you want to continue.

> The start is what stops most people. (Don Shula)

Once you get going, you'll probably keep going. A body at rest tends to stay at rest. A body in motion tends to stay in motion. Fifteen minutes is the precise amount of time needed to turn things around.

John Kenneth Galbraith was a professor of economics at Harvard for fifty years. He was a prolific author. He wrote four dozen books, including several novels, and published more than a thousand articles and essays on various subjects. When asked how he wrote so much, he said,

> All writers know that on some golden mornings they are touched by the wand—are on intimate terms with poetry and cosmic truth. I have experienced those moments myself. Their lesson is simple: It's a total illusion. I am persuaded that most writers, like most shoemakers, are about as good one day as the next. The meaning is that one had better go to his or her typewriter every morning and stay there.

John Kenneth Galbraith found that his writing was just as good on the days that he didn't feel like writing.

> You don't have to be great to start, but you have to start to be great. (Zig Ziglar)

Use the fifteen-minute rule.

Don't Reject Yourself

A female student went up to her college professor after class and asked, "Can I speak to you about graduate school?"

He replied, "Sure." He asked her where she wanted to go.

She replied that she was applying to two small universities in New Jersey.

He asked again where she wanted to go.

Again, she replied that she was applying to two small universities in New Jersey.

The professor said, "But where do you really, really want to go?"

She replied, "Teachers College at Columbia University."

He said, "Apply."

Three years later, he received a voicemail. A female voice said, "I don't know if you remember our conversation about graduate school. I just wanted to let you know that I just received my second master's degree from Teachers College at Columbia University."

Don't reject yourself. Let the university reject you. If you want to go to Harvard, apply to Harvard.

Ask for that date. Apply for that job. Call on that large prospect. If you don't ask, you won't get that date, job, or sale.

The young woman received the advice and applied it. How many times do you receive advice and not follow it?

$$K - A = 0$$

Knowledge minus action equals zero.

The biggest disease in our country is lack of self-esteem. What will other people think? What will other people say?

Well…what will they think or say if you do *nothing*?

You're *Always* Selling Something

You're always selling yourself, your ideas, your report, your project, and your products.

What are you doing when you apply for grad school? Apply for a job? Interview for a job? Interview for a promotion?

What are you doing when you're working on a report? A project? Sending a work-related email?

What are you doing when you apply for a loan?

Life's a competition. Sharpen your skills so that you can win the competition, whether it's impressing a university, a potential employer, your current boss, your clients, your prospects, the loan officer, your coach, or whoever you need to impress daily.

You're in a competition. Sell *yourself!*

Can You Use a Great Sales Formula, Even If You Aren't in Sales?

One hundred percent of all our salaries (directly or indirectly) are dependent on somebody somewhere selling something to somebody at an agreeable price.

The SW formula is a great sales formula, but it can also be helpful to people who don't work in sales. That's because you're always selling yourself.

The SW formula consists of the following:

1. Some will.
2. Some won't.
3. So what!
4. Someone is waiting.
5. Stick with it.
6. Stop worrying.

Some will. Some people will like or even love what you do. That's great if you're in sales, applying for a job, showing your report, starting a website, writing a book, auditioning for a play or a movie, or trying out for a team.

Some won't. Some people will pass on your product, your service, your job skills, your content, your acting skills, or your athletic ability.

So what! You can say, "Woe is me. I never get a break." Or you can keep swinging. One time, Babe Ruth struck out seven times in a doubleheader. A sportswriter said, "Hey, Babe. What do you think about after you strike out?"

Babe replied, "Hitting home runs."

One admirer said that Babe cultivated an "air of indifference." He was going to keep swinging for home runs regardless of what happened previously. During his time, he held the home run records for a season and for a career.

Someone is waiting. Somewhere out there, someone is waiting for what you do. Every time you put yourself out there, you are closer to finding that someone. And that will be exciting!

Stick with it. "Don't quit, can't fail." There are winners and learners. As long as you take the constructive feedback you get and keep moving forward, you will be on the road to success. It may take a while, but you will get there. So keep going!

Stop worrying. You only have a certain amount of control over what people think, whether they love you or hate you. Focus on the power that you do have and that you do control. We control our devotion, our effort, and our attitude. Keep going. Your audience is waiting!

Keep swinging! Keep going!

Rome Wasn't Built in a Day, But...

It's true that Rome wasn't built in a day. But they were laying bricks every day.

Many people focus on the size of their dream or their goal. That can be overwhelming. But you can't get there without laying bricks.

Focus on the process. Start laying bricks.

Make the bricks look as good as you can. And keep going. Your building is ahead of you.

Will Smith says that you don't try to build a wall. You don't set out to make the biggest, greatest wall. You say, "I'm going to lay this brick as perfectly as a brick can be laid." You do this every day, and then before long, you have a wall.

It's difficult to take the first step when you know what the task is. Will says, "The task is never huge to me. It's always one brick. That's what gives me the advantage over people that I'm competing with."

People are paralyzed by getting started. It's the start that stops most people.

Say to yourself, "All I'm doing is laying this one brick. I'm not building the Great Wall of China. I'm going to make this one brick the best brick ever."

Will's father owned a building that was previously used as a bakery. He used the building as his workshop. His father was an electrician and refrigeration man. He installed the long freezer cases in supermarkets. Will and his brother worked every summer with their father installing refrigerator cases. One day, his father decided that he needed a new front wall on his shop. He tore down the front wall, which was about sixteen feet high and thirty feet long. Will and his brother were supposed to build a new front wall. They had to dig a six-foot hole for the foundation. They were mixing the concrete by hand. They were building this wall after school for a year and a half. Will and his brother were the only ones working on the wall. Will said that he can remember standing there, looking at it, and thinking, *There is going to be a hole here forever.* A year and a half later, Will and his brother laid the final brick. Will, his brother, and their father stood back and looked at the wall. Their father said, "Don't y'all ever tell me that you can't do something."

Here's another way to look at it.

A man came upon a construction site where three people were working.

He asked the first, "What are you doing?" and the man answered, "I am laying bricks."

He asked the second, "What are you doing?" and the man answered, "I am building a wall."

He walked up to the third man, who was humming a tune as he worked, and asked, "What are you doing?"

The man stood up, smiled, and said, *"I am building a cathedral."*

A Growth Mindset

In a fixed mindset, students believe their basic abilities, their intelligence, their talents, are just fixed traits. They have a certain amount and that's that, and then their goal becomes to look smart all the time and never look dumb. In a growth mindset, students understand that their talents and abilities can be developed through effort, good teaching, and persistence. They don't necessarily think everyone's the same or anyone can be Einstein, but they believe everyone can get smarter if they work at it.

—Carol Dweck, Stanford University

Dr. Carol Dweck wrote the book *Mindset: The New Psychology of Success*, which should be required reading for everyone.

Why do two people respond to the same situation in different ways? When the game is on the line, one athlete embraces the situation and rises to the occasion. Another athlete chokes. On an airplane, one person is relaxed and looking out the window. Another person is stressed out. They're on the same plane. Life gets in the way, and one person gets off the exercise and nutrition plan, calmly realizes where he or she is, and gets back on track as soon as possible. Another person is crushed and completely goes off track. "I might as well eat this box of cookies. I've blown my fitness goals for this month."

It's the first week of the month! Why can't you get back on track for the next three weeks of the month? Messing up one week doesn't mean you have to blow up the whole month!

Is this just a personality difference or simply a matter of self-discipline?

"Well, I guess that I don't have the grit to keep going when the going gets tough"—saying this to yourself overlooks one of the biggest factors at play, and it's something completely within our control.

You have to be in control of your mindset before you can control your performance. Your mindset is how you see yourself, your situation, and the world. When faced with challenges, your mindset will determine how you respond. One's mindset gets overlooked, but it's one of the most overlooked aspects of performance. You have to master your mindset to unlock your true potential. Your mindset is the difference between reaching your peak potential or cracking under pressure when it matters most. It's the difference between getting decent short-term results and giving up, and being someone who experiences a lifelong transformation. Our mindset is something we can learn to change and improve. This is a truth we have to start believing.

What if you had a plan for dealing with problems so that they wouldn't happen again instead of throwing your hands up in frustration?

What if you could stay calm under pressure, embrace the pressure as a challenge, and still perform your best?

What if you developed plans to redirect your focus when challenges arise and make the best decision to reach your goals?

It's not just possible. With the right tools, it's probable.

Contrary to popular belief, mindset isn't all rah-rah, reading motivational quotes, and thinking positive thoughts. It's a skill that's developed over time with consistent, intentional practice. You have to develop your mental performance just like you develop any other aspect of health, fitness, or performance.

Your mindset can change and grow. That's the first thing that you have to understand. That sounds *so* simple, but this little truth has huge implications.

In her book, social psychologist Carol Dweck uses the terms *fixed* and *growth* when discussing mindsets. Her research has shown that people tend to look at basic qualities like intelligence or talent in two ways:

1. *Fixed (or average).* My intelligence or talent or ability is the way it is, and there's nothing I can do about it. Talent alone creates success, without effort.
2. *Growth (or elite).* My intelligence or talent or ability can be developed through dedication and hard work. Brains and talent are just the starting point.

A growth mindset creates a love of learning and a resilience that is essential for great accomplishment.

This isn't rocket science. It's easy to figure out that having a growth mindset is crucial for success and the foundation for every other aspect of mental performance. You want to train a growth mindset so that you can handle the struggle that you will be faced with when you're pursuing excellence. The belief that you can learn and improve is what you need to make significant, long-term progress even when it's hard. You have to be responsible for the energy, attitude, and mindset that you bring daily.

Do *not* focus on ability as "You either have it or you don't."

Do focus on the effort that you put in and how much you've learned and developed through the work you've invested.

Never say, "I messed up again. I guess I just don't have the discipline to stick with it. It's just who I am. I don't have what it takes."

Do say, "I hit a snag here, but I *can* learn the skills and strategies I need to improve."

Do say, "This isn't the end of the road. It's just a bend in the road."

It may seem small, but having a growth mindset empowers you to believe that you're in control of your ability. You can learn and improve. This is the key to success in academics, athletics, business, marriage, and life. This is crucial for your long-term success.

Brian Cain, the Peak Mental Performance coach to athletes, coaches, and executives, posted the following on BrianCain.com.

AVERAGE MINDSET
ELITE MINDSET

PEOPLE WITH AN AVERAGE MINDSET:

FEEL SORRY FOR THEMSELVES

SEE CONFIDENCE AS A FEELING

MAKE AN EXCUSE

SAY IT'S IMPOSSIBLE

FOCUS ON HOW THEY FEEL

USE THE PHRASE HAVE TO

WEAR THEIR EMOTIONS ON THEIR SLEEVES

SEE FAILURE AS FINAL

FOCUS ON WHAT THEY CAN'T CONTROL

PEOPLE WITH AN ELITE MINDSET:

ARE SO FOCUSED ON OTHERS THAT THEY DON'T HAVE TIME TO FEEL SORRY FOR THEMSELVES

KNOW CONFIDENCE IS AN ACTION

MAKE IT HAPPEN

SAY IT'S GOING TO BE VERY DIFFICULT

FOCUS ON HOW THEY ACT AND WHAT THEY NEED TO DO

USE THE PHRASE GET TO OR WANT TO

NEVER SHOW WEAKNESS AND ARE BIG WITH THEIR BODY LANGUAGE

SEE FAILURE AS POSITIVE FEEDBACK

FOCUS ON WHAT THEY CAN CONTROL

If

If you can keep your head when all about you
Are losing theirs and blaming it on you,
If you can trust yourself when all men doubt you,
But make allowance for their doubting too;
If you can wait and not be tired by waiting,
Or being lied about, don't deal in lies,
Or being hated, don't give way to hating,
And yet don't look too good, nor talk too wise;

If you can dream—and not make dreams your master;
If you can think—and not make thoughts your aim;
If you can meet with Triumph and Disaster
And treat those two impostors just the same;
If you can bear to hear the truth you've spoken
Twisted by knaves to make a trap for fools,
Or watch the things you gave your life to, broken,
And stoop and build 'em up with worn-out tools;

If you can make one heap of all your winnings
And risk it on one turn of pitch-and-toss,
And lose, and start again at your beginnings
And never breathe a word about your loss;
If you can force your heart and nerve and sinew
To serve your turn long after they are gone,
And so hold on when there is nothing in you
Except the Will which says to them: "Hold on!";

If you can talk with crowds and keep your virtue,
Or walk with Kings—nor lose the common touch,
If neither foes nor loving friends can hurt you,
If all men count with you, but none too much;
If you can fill the unforgiving minute
With sixty seconds' worth of distance run,
Yours is the Earth and everything that's in it,
And—which is more—you'll be a Man, my son!

—Rudyard Kipling, "If—"

I don't think I can go through a year without thinking of the words in "If." I was watching an NBA playoff game one day. One team was losing their poise, pointing fingers, and blaming teammates. The other team clearly relished the opportunity to be in that situation. I thought, *If you can keep your head when everyone around you is losing theirs and blaming it on you, you'll be a man, my son!*

Sometimes I will walk into a customer's store, and immediately they'll start telling me about a problem with a product or an invoice. Then I have to call the company I represent and speak for my customer. At first, the person in the corporate office will say that I'm wrong. There couldn't be a problem with the product or the invoice. I have to keep my cool to work things out while there is a person by me with one problem and a person on the phone with another problem.

If you can keep your head when everyone around you is losing theirs and blaming it on you…

"I'll call the office."

The Man Who Thinks He Can

By Walter D. Wintle

Attitude is everything!

If you think you are beaten, you are;
If you think you dare not, you don't.
If you'd like to win, but think you can't
It's almost a cinch you won't.

If you think you'll lose, you've lost.
For out in the world we find
Success begins with a fellow's will:
It's all in his state of mind.

If you think you're outclassed, you are:
You've got to think high to rise,
You've got to be sure of yourself before
You'll ever win that prize.

Life's battles don't always go
To the stronger or faster man,
But sooner or later the man who wins
Is the one who thinks he can.

You Still Should

A young woman was in the kitchen, talking to her nine-year-old son. She was telling him how she had a dream to write children's books. But she had been so busy with her church work and raising two children that she never had written a book.

Her son said, "Mom, you still should."

Those words from her son stuck in her mind—"You still should."

So she started writing books. Now she has written several best-sellers. Do you have a dream to write a book? You still should.

Do you have a dream to start a business, create a website, go to grad school, apply for a new job, or apply for a promotion? You still should.

It's not too late to get started on a dream or a goal. Everything hasn't been done. Nobody has done it with your experiences and your point of view.

You may have put it off for a year or for twenty-five years, but you're not too old or too young. You haven't missed your window of opportunity. Get busy moving toward your destiny.

You tried before, and it didn't work out. People are telling you it never will work out. Every setback means that you're one step closer. Thomas Edison had to try one thousand times before he invented the light bulb.

If you're not passionate about your job or your career, you need to be in a field that matches your gifts and your talents. Don't spend your whole life in the wrong career.

Start taking steps toward your dream, even if they're small steps.

Make the rest of your life the best of your life. Dream bigger. Act wiser. Get out of your comfort zone. Complacency kills.

This is a new day. This is your time. This is your moment. Share your gift with the world. Now.

You still should.

I May Not Understand Your Problems, But...

You might be thinking, *But, Don, you don't understand my problems.* I probably don't understand your problems. But you probably don't understand mine either.

When I open my mouth, I get a look like "What's wrong with him?" I've had to learn to overcome that by showing sincerity. People can tell that I know what I want to say but am having trouble saying it, so they try harder to understand me. It's not an easy thing to do. First, I had to understand what people were thinking. I was in a support group for a while until we ran out of topics. I've read about spasmodic dysphonia, which affects my vocal cords. I've listened to interviews with people who have SD. I've talked with people who have SD. I learned that people think we're sick, nervous, scared, drunk, crazy, or that we've had a stroke. How would you like to get that every time you open your mouth?

A guy told me that my phone was breaking up.

I said, "My voice is breaking up." And I laughed.

He tried harder to understand me.

Even when I'm talking to somebody and having to repeat myself often, that person will say, "Give me a call." People can't imagine that talking on the phone is difficult for someone. At a spasmodic dysphonia support group meeting, if you say that talking on the phone is the worst thing, everybody in the room will laugh and nod their head. They know. Companies will say, "Now voice–activated," and I'd be like, "Oh no. Now the machine will tell me that it can't understand me." I would rather just punch a number for the department or for what I'm calling about. I need to talk to a real person. And hopefully, it's a patient person.

I know people with the same voice disorder who have retired because of it. Yet, I'm *still* working in sales.

Fifteen years after developing a voice disorder, I started pioneering a new line in this area. At first, I was selling it to my old customers. Then I started going to places I had never been before. They had never heard of me nor the company I'm representing. Now, the owner of the company told me that it was okay for me to expand my territory to two new cities because I'm opening new accounts and nobody is working those two cities.

I've had to adjust.

I have to repeat things and rephrase things all the time. I've learned to stay calm and composed until they understand what I'm saying. People actually start to respect me more because I'm going to keep trying until they understand what I say.

Fortunately, I can use email more now and mail out cards that I make on a website. But the first contact is always to meet the prospect in person and show him or her what we can create for their business. And then they end up thanking me for the new custom products we created for them to sell.

I'm learning, growing, and staying in the game! And in my second year representing the new line, I made more money with the new line than I made with the two lines I had been representing for more than twenty years.

Stay in the game *no matter what*. People will respect you more for working to overcome a problem than they will for complaining about a problem!

I talked with a man who played for five NBA teams during his fifteen-year career. I asked him what his mindset was when he had to adjust to a new town, new coaches, and new teammates. He held his hands by his eyes, like a horse with blinders on, and he said, "I was focused on what I needed to do." And he repeated that. "I was focused on what I needed to do."

I asked, "What you needed to do here and now?"

He replied, "Yes. I got traded. I wasn't going to cry about it. I focused on where I was *now*."

And he stayed in the league for fifteen years!

> I am not afraid of storms, for I am learning
> how to sail my ship. (*Little Women*)

The Incredible Story of Victoria Arlen

At age eleven, Victoria Arlen started experiencing pain in her side. Before long, it led to her body shutting down. For three and a half years, she couldn't speak or move; she was trapped in her body.

Two rare neurological conditions ravaged her body. Doctors said she wouldn't be anything for the rest of her life. If she survived, she would be in a vegetative state for the rest of her life.

She was alive but couldn't communicate with anybody. She thought, *God, you're the only one who can hear me. I'm going to be talking to you a lot.*

In 2009, her mother saw her blink. She asked Victoria to blink twice if she could hear her. Victoria blinked twice. So, finally, she could communicate with her family by blinking twice for yes and once for no. She had to learn to move her eyes to track things. She had to learn to speak. She had to learn to move her arms.

She missed five years of school but wanted to graduate with her triplet brothers. They thought that she was nuts, but she was determined to do it.

She entered the tenth grade with a fifth-grade education. She did graduate with her brothers in 2013.

Before her illness, Victoria had been very active in sports. She really loved swimming. In 2010, she found the water again. It wasn't by choice. Her brothers strapped a life jacket on her, picked her up, and jumped into a swimming pool. She was traumatized. She hadn't been able to move for years, and here she was in the water. It changed her life.

She said that when things in life scare you, you literally or figuratively need to jump in and get over that fear and go after it.

She learned how to swim again, without using her legs. She found a freedom that she didn't have on land. She didn't need a wheelchair. She didn't need help. She could just be in the water.

Nobody needed to know her story. Nobody needed to know that she had to remove a feeding tube before she got into the water. Nobody could tell. She was normal again when she was in the water.

She set her sights on the London Paralympic Games in 2012. Nobody gave her a chance. She was coming into this Paralympic sport late in life. Most of her peers were training in 2008, while Victoria was fighting for her life. Her coach and her family believed in her, and it worked out pretty well. She won a gold medal and three silver medals in the 2012 London Paralympic Games.

She was asked how she continued when it seemed like she had nothing to live for. How did she smile when it seemed like she should just curl up into a ball and cry?

She came up with a motto because she wanted a second chance. She told herself, "Face it. Embrace it. Defy it. Conquer it."

Face it head-on. She couldn't run away. Accept it.

Embrace it because she couldn't be angry or bitter. That solves nothing. Life happens. Things happen. We can't explain it.

Defy the odds that she couldn't do it. The doctors said that she wouldn't survive or would be a vegetable. The coaches said that she couldn't make it.

Conquer it. Doctors and coaches said she wouldn't do it. It's so easy to squash someone's dreams. A lot of people told her no, but a handful of people said that she could. She held on to that.

In 2013, she stood on her own two feet again. She started learning to walk again.

Since then, she has worked for ESPN as a reporter and host. She has been on *Dancing with the Stars*. Now she is doing ads and catalog covers for Jockey, in her underwear.

She said that our mindset and our mental attitude influence our results. It can make our lives better, and ultimately, it can get us out of the darkest hours of our life.

On YouTube, watch "Face It. Embrace It. Defy It. Conquer It: Victoria Arlen at TEDx Amoskeag Millyard." This was recorded in November 2013 when she was in a wheelchair.

Watch her in 2018 in Jockey underwear on YouTube, "Show 'Em What's Underneath: Victoria Arlen."

Our Deepest Fear

Poem by Marianne Williamson

Our deepest fear is not that we are inadequate.
Our deepest fear is that we are powerful beyond measure.
It is our light, not our darkness
That most frightens us.
We ask ourselves
Who am I to be brilliant, gorgeous, talented, fabulous?
Actually, who are you not to be?
You are a child of God. You're playing small does not serve the world.
There's nothing enlightened about shrinking
So that other people won't feel insecure around you.
We are all meant to shine, as children do.
We were born to make manifest the glory of God that is within us.
It's not just in some of us; it's in everyone.
And as we let our own light shine,
We unconsciously give other people permission to do the same.
As we're liberated from our own fear,
Our presence automatically liberates others.

The Champion Creed

We think that people should be perfect and never lose, but winners lose more than losers do.

Every year in Major League Baseball, the Cy Young Award is awarded to the best pitcher in each league. Cy Young holds the record for the most wins by a pitcher. He also holds the record for the most losses by a pitcher.

At one time, Babe Ruth held the record for the most home runs hit, and he also held the record for the most strikeouts by a batter. After striking out seven times in a doubleheader, a reporter asked Ruth what he thought about after striking out.

Babe replied, "Hitting home runs."

Pete Rose set the record for the most hits. Before he set that record, he set the record for the most outs made.

Nolan Ryan holds the record for the most strikeouts by a pitcher. Years before he set the strikeout record, Ryan set the record for the most batters walked by a pitcher.

Before Tom Hopkins became a world-class salesman and a great sales trainer, he struggled with self-image problems. Once he decided to become a salesman, he talked to other salespeople and attended seminars. He soaked up all the advice he could but still hadn't improved his self-image. He finally realized that the encouragement to keep working had to come from within. He started writing down what he would like to hear from a mentor or coach on those days when everything he touched was turning into something that wasn't gold. The following is what he came up with.

> I am not judged by the number of times
> that I fail, but by the number of times I succeed.
> And the number of times I succeed is in direct
> proportion to the number of times I can fail and
> keep trying.

Tom wrote this creed and put it where he'd see it multiple times a day. Later, he used this creed in every seminar he taught. You can print a PDF at this website: http://www.tomhopkins.com/pdf/PrintChampionCreed.pdf. Take it and use it so that you can keep trying until you achieve your dreams.

There are winners and learners. It's not over unless you give up. If you look at each situation as a learning experience, it's much more likely that you will end up winning.

We look at someone who has succeeded, and we only see their success and think that it came easily for them. We don't look at all the failure their success is built on. Then we think that we have to avoid failure.

Instead, we need to look at the failures that led to the successes of Hall of Famers like Cy Young, Babe Ruth, Pete Rose, and Nolan Ryan.

Rejection is part of the territory for salespeople—yet Tom Hopkins overcame self-image problems and learned to build his self-esteem and find the resilience to bounce back from failure. And he became a great salesman and a great sales trainer.

Stay strong. Push past obstacles and failures. Become a champion!

Blow Your Own Horn in Job Interviews

This quote is from author and speaker Susan Sontag: "Descriptions mean nothing without examples."

Stories stick. Stories are memorable. Stories change lives. Everything in sports, TV, movies, and newspapers is a story.

Think about Disneyland, Disney World, and Harry Potter. Those are stories. Jesus told parables. Those are stories. Eighty percent of the Bible is stories.

If you get a job interview, you're in a competition. How are you going to stand out from the others?

Show, don't tell. Facts tell. Stories sell.

If you were interviewing to be a writer on a comedy show, don't tell me you're funny. Make me laugh.

Show me by telling stories about what you did.

What have you done? If you've won awards, tell about it.

If you work well with groups, what did you and your group do? If you improved something, what did you improve?

One year, I opened at least one new account every week for fifty consecutive weeks. I put that on my résumé for every job interview after that. And the interviewer always noticed that.

They don't want to hire someone who will just keep the territory where it is. They want someone who will expand the business in that territory.

Opening new accounts will increase business. And it showed that I wasn't just sitting on the account list that I'd been given. I was looking for new accounts.

You might be thinking that it's not your style to blow your own horn, but if you're in a job interview, who else is going to tell your story?

Now is the time to tell your own story.

The Time I Didn't Blow My Own Horn in a Job Interview

I started as a sales representative in menswear by training with two sales reps in the Houston area. I'd spend one week with the sales rep who had the major accounts and one week with the sales rep who had the small accounts. The major-accounts rep had me take inventory in department stores, and I even wrote up some of the orders. Then I spent the summer covering a territory that included all of Colorado and Wyoming, the panhandle of Nebraska, and a few counties in New Mexico. At the end of the summer, they hired a full-time rep for that territory, and I spent some time going over things with him.

Then our district manager resigned. They promoted the major-accounts rep in Houston to district manager. It's highly unusual for your first territory to be the major-accounts territory; however, I knew all of the buyers in the major-accounts territory in Houston, and I had helped work up the orders.

Also, my wife and I had an apartment in Houston, so they didn't have to pay to move someone. And I had spent three months traveling in four states I had never been to before, getting orders there.

I spent about four years working the major-accounts territory in Houston and won district and regional sales contests. The regional award was a trip for me and my wife to the Super Bowl in Miami. All of the department stores in Houston had buying offices in Houston. This was when department stores were expanding and opening new stores. Also, I sold to the largest sporting goods chain in the country at that time, which was headquartered in Houston.

Then I worked as a sales rep in sporting goods for three years and continued to sell to the largest sporting goods chain in the country. I won a national sales contest during this time. There was a guy from my hometown that I'd see at sporting goods shows. He represented a hot line of athletic shoes. The shoes had a gimmick that had caught on with athletes and schoolchildren. He told me they needed a sales rep in South Texas. I sent them my résumé, and I got an interview.

I drove to Dallas and spent a night at my mother's house. Then I drove to a small town in Arkansas and spent a night there before my interview the next morning. There were two guys who interviewed me. They seemed pleasant. I don't remember ever feeling uncomfortable during the interview. But they kept asking me if I had worked along the Texas border with Mexico. At the time, I hadn't. After I left the sporting goods industry, I represented three eyewear companies and covered the southern half of Texas for seven years, including the border from Laredo to Brownsville. (I really enjoyed working the border. Every business is bilingual, and the people were so nice. It seemed like a vacation to me.) So I kept saying that I hadn't worked along the border. I thought that everything had gone well, except for the fact that they kept bringing up that I hadn't worked along the border. My father's parents lived in South Texas when I was growing up, so I wasn't worried about working there.

About a week later, I got a letter thanking me for the interview but stating that they had decided not to hire me because I didn't have experience along the border, and I didn't have experience with department stores. The border part I could understand, but department stores? I was thinking, *What? How did that happen?* I had four years' experience selling to every department store in Houston and had won district and regional sales contests during that time. I had seven years' experience selling to the largest sporting goods chain in the country. How could somebody say that I didn't have experience with major accounts?

After thinking about it, I didn't remember even talking about department stores. I just remember them going on and on about working on the border. I guess I was waiting for them to ask me about department stores, and I never brought it up in the interview. Based on my experience at that time, that should have been the first thing that I brought up!

In the whole scheme of things, I'm *not* upset that I didn't get the job with that shoe company. The fad for their gimmick started fading out. They were out of business by the end of the decade. I would have been getting in at the tail end of their success, and it would have been all downhill from there.

But I learned a valuable lesson.
If I don't blow my own horn in an interview,
who will know what I've done?

Show How Your Past Jobs Prepared You for a New Job

If you are changing industries or seeking a promotion, connect what you've been doing to the job you are seeking.

After graduating from college, I worked in retail stores for six years. I managed the men's and boys' departments in department stores and worked with the buyers. Then I managed a men's store and did the buying. So in interviews to be a sales representative, I stressed that I was the type of person that wholesale companies sell to, and I had worked in both department stores and small independent stores.

After working in menswear, I interviewed to be a sales rep in sporting goods. I stressed that I had been selling to retail stores, from department stores to independent stores, and I had won district and regional sales contests.

After working in sporting goods, I interviewed with an eyewear company. I stressed that I had been selling to the largest sporting goods chain in the country and to small independent stores, and I had won a national sales contest.

While I had no experience selling to optical shops or optometrists, I pointed out that I had worn eyeglasses since I was six. So I had been a consumer of eyeglass frames for a long time.

After working in eyewear, I interviewed with a souvenir company. I stressed that I had been selling to retail stores for decades and I had opened at least one new account for fifty consecutive weeks while selling eyewear.

After working in souvenirs for a long time, I got the opportunity to represent a company that makes custom apparel. I pointed out that I had been selling some custom items for the two companies I was representing at that time.

If you are seeking a promotion within your company or a job with a new company, there is something that you have been doing that prepared you for that next level.

"Have you done this before?" Turn that into a chance to tell how your past experience will help you sell to people or supervise people in the job you're seeking.

"Besides being 'smarter than the average bear,'
what other qualifications do you have?"

This Is What Impressed Steve Jobs in a Job Interview

Ever wish you knew what your boss is really thinking?

Steve Jobs believed that one quality mattered much, much more than the résumé, the clothes, or answering tricky interview questions. After hiring a few professional managers, he learned that "most of them were bozos. They knew how to manage, but they didn't know how to do anything." So Jobs began to look for a different trait. He said, "We wanted people that were insanely great at what they did but were not necessarily those seasoned professionals but who had, at the tips of their fingers and in their passion, the latest understanding of where technology was and what they could do with that technology." Instead of job experience, Steve Jobs wanted to hire passionate, enthusiastic people who would manage themselves, understand the company's mission, and strive for the common goal. Instead of a normal job interview, the Apple team would present job candidates with a Macintosh prototype and take note of their reactions. If their eyes lit up and they got really excited, the Apple team "knew they were one of us."

This doesn't just work at Apple. Look around at offices, stores, restaurants, auto repair shops, or any other place you go. How many people are just in their jobs, and how many people are really into it? The ones who are really into it will stand out wherever they are. This works in school, business, sales, research, and marriage.

Steve Madden, the founder of Steve Madden Ltd. (the company that designs and markets shoes and fashion accessories for women,

men, and children), was asked what advice he would give to young people just starting out.

He replied, "When you go to work, do what you love to do. Don't do it for the money. Do it because you love doing it. Then the money will follow."

Do what you love. Love what you do.

Jeff Bezos said he wants to hire people at Amazon who will listen—not strategic listening, where you're thinking about what you're going to say, but actually absorbing what you're being told.

After representing a line of high-priced eyewear and a line of medium-priced eyewear for two years, I interviewed with a company that sold low-priced eyewear. Shortly after the interview started, he laid down my résumé and said, "Let's talk about frames [for eyeglasses] instead." He started showing me his samples and telling me the prices.

I asked, "How do you sell these frames at this price?" That was an honest reaction on my part, but he knew at that point that I liked what he was showing me and, more importantly, that I would be able to sell his line. I got the job.

Enthusiasm impressed Steve Jobs in a job interview.
You can use this in every job interview.
Real enthusiasm works.

You're Not a Chicken; You're an Eagle

Once, there was an eagle that was born in a chicken coop. As he grew up, all he ever saw was chickens. So he walked like a chicken, pecked like a chicken, and ate like a chicken. That's all he knew.

One day, he looked up in the sky and saw an eagle soaring through the air. Something inside him said, "That's what I'm supposed to be."

He looked around and realized that he wasn't built like a chicken. His wings were broader, longer, and stronger.

He told his chicken buddies that he was going to soar like that eagle. The chickens all laughed at him and said, "You're a chicken. That's all you've ever been."

The eagle ignored the chickens and started trying to learn how to use his wings better. He flapped his wings as hard as he could, and he lifted himself up and flew. But he flew right into the side of the chicken coop.

The chickens all laughed and said, "We told you that you were a chicken."

Nevertheless, the eagle was persistent. He kept trying. Then, one day, he took off and was soaring high over the chicken coop. He thought, *This is what I'm supposed to do. I'm* not *a chicken!*

*****

There was a young lady who was raised in government housing by a single mom. She was left alone a lot because her mother was working different jobs. But she kept thinking that she was going to get a college degree so that she could get a better job and wouldn't have to live in government housing.

However, when she was sixteen, she got pregnant and had to drop out of school to take care of her son. She got a small apartment and tried to make ends meet. She couldn't do it and had to go on welfare. It looked like she was going to have the same type of life as her mother and other family members.

She got a job punching meal tickets in a school. She decided to take classes at night and got her GED in two years.

She still wasn't satisfied, so she continued to take classes at night. In four years, she graduated from college with honors.

She still wasn't satisfied, so she went on to earn a master's degree.

Now she is the assistant principal at the same school where she used to punch meal tickets.

She said that she had been on welfare, but now she was "fair and well."

*****

You may be surrounded by chickens. Everybody may be telling you that you're a chicken. Your relatives may think that they're chickens. But you've got more inside you. You're not a chicken.

You were made to soar like an eagle.

You Can Handle It

A businessman had worked for a home improvement company for thirty years. He had helped develop it into a nationwide company. However, there was a corporate restructuring, and they decided they didn't need him anymore. He didn't hang his head and whine, "Why me?" Instead, he got together with a few friends, and they formed their own home improvement company. They named it Home Depot. Of course, Home Depot is now one of the largest home improvement companies in the world.

A setback is a setup for a comeback. Use what you've learned and keep moving forward. Don't be a weakling. Be a warrior!

There was a very wealthy man who was also very eccentric. In his pool, he had sharks and alligators. At a party in his backyard, he announced to his guests that if anyone would swim across the pool, he would give that person anything he or she wanted. Soon after his announcement, there was a loud splash. He saw a man swimming at ninety miles per hour across the pool, avoiding the sharks and swimming around the alligators.

When the guest hopped out of the pool, the wealthy man said, "You're the bravest man I've ever seen. What can I give you?"

The guest replied, "The thing that I want more than anything else is to know the name of the person who pushed me into the pool."

You may have been pushed into the pool. It might have been unexpected. It might have been unfair.

But you can handle it.
Do like the owners of Home Depot, and create your own destiny!

Everything You Need Is Inside You

Everything you need is already inside you. You aren't lacking intelligence, creativity, focus, motivation, or whatever it is you need to succeed. You're blocking it.

In 1501, Michelangelo was searching for a large piece of marble, about fifteen feet tall. He finally found a piece that another sculptor had discarded. For three years, he chipped away at it. In 1504, he unveiled the statue of David, which has been called the greatest sculpture of all time. Michelangelo was asked how he created such a magnificent sculpture. He replied that David was already in the marble. He just had to chip away everything that wasn't David.

It's the same with you. Everything you need is already inside you. You aren't lacking it. You're blocking it. You have to chip away the blocks, the rationalization, and the misconceptions. A great artist, a great student, a great salesperson, or a great entrepreneur is inside you.

You have to chip away everything that's not you.
Start chipping right now!

Four Quotes to Remember

I want to leave you with four quotes.

I've learned that people will forget what you said, people will forget what you did, but people will never forget how you made them feel. (Maya Angelou)

Nobody cares how much you know until they know how much you care. (Theodore Roosevelt)

You should treat others the way you want to be treated yourself. (*The Golden Rule*)

It's all about others. (Dr. Rob Gilbert, *Success Hotline*)

Final Words

I hope this book gave you some ideas so that you can create an exciting new start in your life.